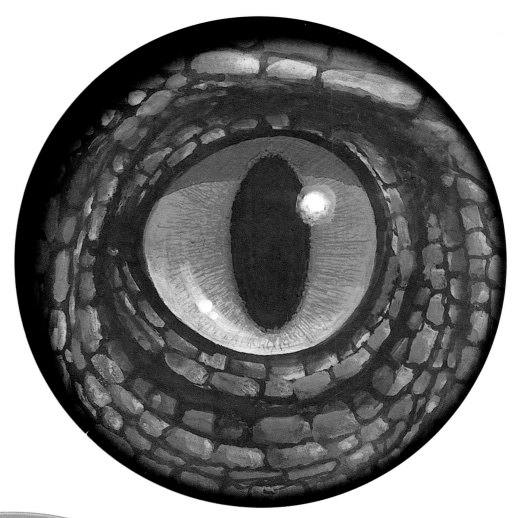

LIFE-SIZE DINOSAURS

David Bergen

STERLING PUBLISHING CO., INC.
NEW YORK

First published in the UK in 2004 by
Chrysalis Children's Books
an imprint of Chrysalis Books Group plc

Library of Congress Cataloging-in-Publication
Data Available

10 9 8 7 6 5 4 3 2 1

Published in 2004 by Sterling Publishing Co., Inc.
387 Park Avenue South, New York, NY 10016

Distributed in Canada by Sterling Publishing
c/o Canadian Manda Group,
165 Dufferin Street
Toronto, Ontario, Canada M6K 3H6

Editorial Director Honor Head
Senior Editors Sarah Walker, Rasha Elsaeed
Project Editor Jean Coppendale
Text, illustration and design David Bergen
Consultant Dougal Dixon
Additional design Simon Rosenheim, Alix Wood
Cover designer Sophie Wilkins

ISBN 1-4027-3039-X

WHAT ARE DINOSAURS?

Dinosaurs are animals that appeared on Earth two hundred and thirty million years ago, before mysteriously disappearing sixty-five million years ago. Some were enormous, fierce meat eaters, others small vegetarians. What else do we know about them?

Dinosaur family tree

We divide dinosaurs into two main groups or families, as shown below. The Saurischia (lizard-hipped) includes giant, meat-eating theropods such as *Tyrannosaurus*, as well as plant-eating sauropods such as *Diplodocus*. The Ornithischia (bird-hipped) group includes all plant eaters, such as *Stegosaurus* and *Triceratops*.

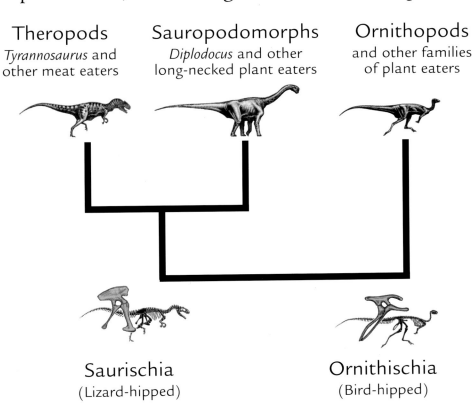

Theropods	Sauropodomorphs	Ornithopods
Tyrannosaurus and other meat eaters	*Diplodocus* and other long-necked plant eaters	and other families of plant eaters

Saurischia
(Lizard-hipped)

Ornithischia
(Bird-hipped)

Holey head

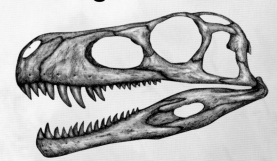

Another clue that helps us to identify a dinosaur fossil from that of another animal is the holes found in the skull behind the eyes. The holes in this *Herrerasaurus* skull are shown clear (above). Holes made the skull lighter and more flexible. They made room for the jaw muscles to be effective in tearing up food. For this reason meat eaters, with the largest holes, had massive jaw muscles.

Helpful hips?

All dinosaurs had a hole in their hip socket as a result of the way they walked. Dinosaurs had upright legs, held straight beneath them, instead of sprawled out to the side like other reptiles, such as crocodiles and lizards. This hip hole helps paleontologists (dinosaur scientists) to distinguish dinosaur and non-dinosaur fossils.

Dinosaur Age

The time of the dinosaurs is known as the MESOZOIC ERA. This is divided into three periods: the CRETACEOUS (144-65 million years ago), the JURASSIC (206-144 million years ago) and the TRIASSIC (248-206 million years ago).

How it all began...

More than two hundred and forty million years ago, some ten million years before the first dinosaurs, a small, meat-eating reptile roamed the Earth. This was *Euparkeria* – possibly the ancestor of all dinosaurs and modern-day crocodiles.

Euparkeria walked mostly on four legs. But it could also run quickly after its prey on its two back legs.

Early hunters

The dawn of the dinosaur age began about two hundred and forty-eight million years ago. The Earth was mostly dry desert, but the south was a more fertile area, full of green forests. These forests were the hunting grounds of two of the earliest known dinosaurs, *Eoraptor* (Dawn thief) and *Herrerasaurus* (Herrera's reptile). *Eoraptor* was a small, agile meat eater. *Herrerasaurus* was three times larger with long, hind legs. Remains of these two dinosaurs have been found close by each other, and alongside other, early dinosaurs. This has led some scientists to call this area (which now forms part of South America) "the cradle of dinosauria".

Eoraptor and Herrerasaurus

The first killers

Herrerasaurus (top) and *Eoraptor* (bottom) were bipedal dinosaurs. This means they walked upright on their back legs. In fact, all meat-eating dinosaurs were bipedal. This made them agile hunters as it meant that their front legs were free for other tasks, such as gripping prey with sharp claws. *Herrerasaurus* was also the first known carnivorous dinosaur to develop a special locking joint in the lower jaw. This gave its bite an extra strong grip, so there would be no easy escape for its unfortunate prey!

Contents

The skeletons of an adult human, Herrerasaurus *and the smaller* Eoraptor, *shown to the same scale.*

LIFE-SIZE

The LIFE SIZE stamp

This stamp shows which dinosaurs and other animals are illustrated as life size in this book. On some pages, the dinosaurs appear at different stages in their lives – the *Tyrannosaurus* teeth on page 15 are enormous, but they would have grown even bigger as the dinosaur grew older! On other pages, the "life-size" dinosaurs and animals are reconstructed from the measurements of their fossils. When the pictures of fossils are the same size as the fossil remains they are also shown with a "Life Size" stamp. When animal skeletons are shown, an adult human skeleton is included to give a sense of scale. When an animal or fossil is shown on a smaller scale, the size of an adult hand shows how large it is.

Not a dinosaur!

Saurosuchus wasn't a dinosaur and, although it may look like it, it wasn't a crocodile either! It belonged to a group of reptiles called rauisuchians, which ruled the world just as the first dinosaurs were appearing. *Saurosuchus* was a huge carnivore, measuring about 7 meters (23 feet) from nose to tail. Its great skull was 1 meter (3 feet) long. As the dinosaurs became more established, the rauisuchians started to die out. By the end of the Triassic Period they were extinct. We don't know why this happened.

DINOSAUR PLANET

Two hundred and twenty million years ago the Triassic world was one huge supercontinent called Pangaea (meaning "all earth"). The continents as we know them today were joined together, and so the world looked completely different.

United Earth

On the globe (right) you can see how the seven modern continents (Europe, North and South America, Africa, Asia, Antarctica and Australia) formed the western half of Pangaea. Such a huge land mass meant that the climate changed very little from year-to-year. It also prevented the world-wide flow of ocean currents that we have today. As there was only one long coastline, the variety of sea life was quite limited.

The supercontinent of Pangaea.

All change!

By the late Triassic Period, when the dinosaurs had become established, Pangaea began to break up. Over the next two hundred million years pieces of this gigantic "jigsaw puzzle" continued to drift apart until they formed the lands we know today.

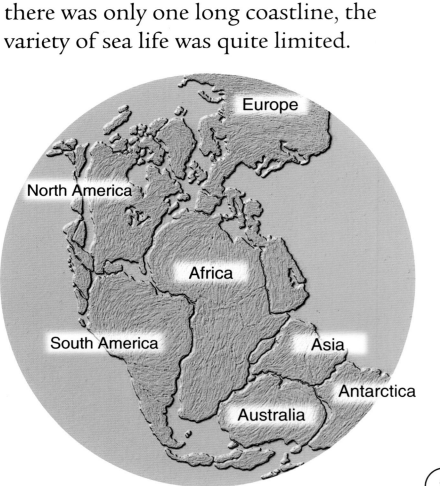

Here you can see how the pieces of the Pangaea "puzzle" fitted together. Today's continents are marked in their positions two hundred million years ago.

The first chewers

Ornithopods (bird-footed dinosaurs) from the Cretaceous Period included the *Iguanodon* and later the "duck-billed" hadrosaurs. Ornithopods had moveable bones in their skulls that crunched their jaws together in a grinding action. They also had comb-like rows of "self-sharpening" teeth. Their fleshy cheeks held the food while the jaws chewed.

Parrot Beak

The ceratopsians (Horned faces) had self-sharpening teeth and the strongest jaws of all plant-eating dinosaurs. An early type of ceratopsian, *Psittacosaurus* (Parrot reptile), had a strong, beak-like mouth that it used for cropping the tough vegetation of the dry Cretaceous deserts. It used gastroliths, too.

Turtles (the smaller skull below the Psittacosaurus skull) are reptiles that also have a horn beak.

Beak face

Ornithopods developed a very efficient way of eating. They cropped plants and leaves from the trees with their tough, horn "beak", and then used their leaf-shaped teeth to crush the plants.

Dryosaurus (Oak lizard) was a beak-faced ornithopod. It measured about 3 meters (10 feet) long and stood 1.7 meters (5 feet) tall.

Veggie herders

Herds of dryosaurs probably roamed widely across the Jurassic plains in search of plant life. Fossils of *Dryosaurus* have been found as far apart as North America and East Africa. They would have been preyed upon by fierce meat eaters such as allosaurus.

THE MEAT EATERS

Most carnivores had very similar teeth: sharp, serrated and shaped like daggers. They were all used for the same purpose – gripping on to prey, and tearing and ripping flesh from bone!

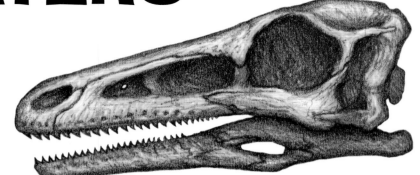

The skull of Troodon *has exactly one hundred teeth.*

Clever killer

Troodon means "Wounding tooth", and the saw-edged teeth of this late Cretaceous Period meat eater would certainly have put a quick end to its prey. Although it wasn't a big animal, *Troodon* had a large brain for its size, and is considered to have been one of the more intelligent dinosaurs. It lived in packs, and its large eyes mean that it probably hunted at dawn and at dusk.

Troodon *tooth*

Needle teeth

Compsognathus (Elegant jaw) lived on a group of islands which lay in the warm, late Jurassic sea, in the region that is now Europe. Although not much larger than a chicken, *Compsognathus* was a fierce predator. It had needle-sharp teeth that it would have used to grip its struggling prey. One fossil specimen has even been found with a lizard inside – the fossilized remains of its last meal. Like *Troodon*, little *Compsognathus* had large eyes for its size, which might be an indication of its intelligence – or show that it hunted at night.

SHARED WORLD

Many different animals shared the dinosaurs' world. Some of them you would recognize today. There were frogs and lizards, crocodiles and turtles, as well as small mammals. Sharks swam in the oceans – and in the rivers! Many fierce and now extinct swimming reptiles ruled the seas. Birds began to appear only in the late Jurassic Period. Before them, the skies belonged to flying insects, and to winged predators known as the pterosaurs.

Finely preserved

This picture is of a fossil of a dragonfly that was around at the same time as the small pterosaur, *Pterodactylus* (below). It lived in the lagoons in the warm, late Jurassic sea where Germany is today.

LIFE-SIZE

Pterodactylus

This life-size picture of *Pterodactylus*, and the skulls of three different kinds of pterodactyls (seen here actual size), show how delicate these small pterosaurs were. These tiny creatures must have been expert flyers and this, together with signs in some fossils of a downy, hair-like covering, suggests that they may have been warm blooded, like mammals today.

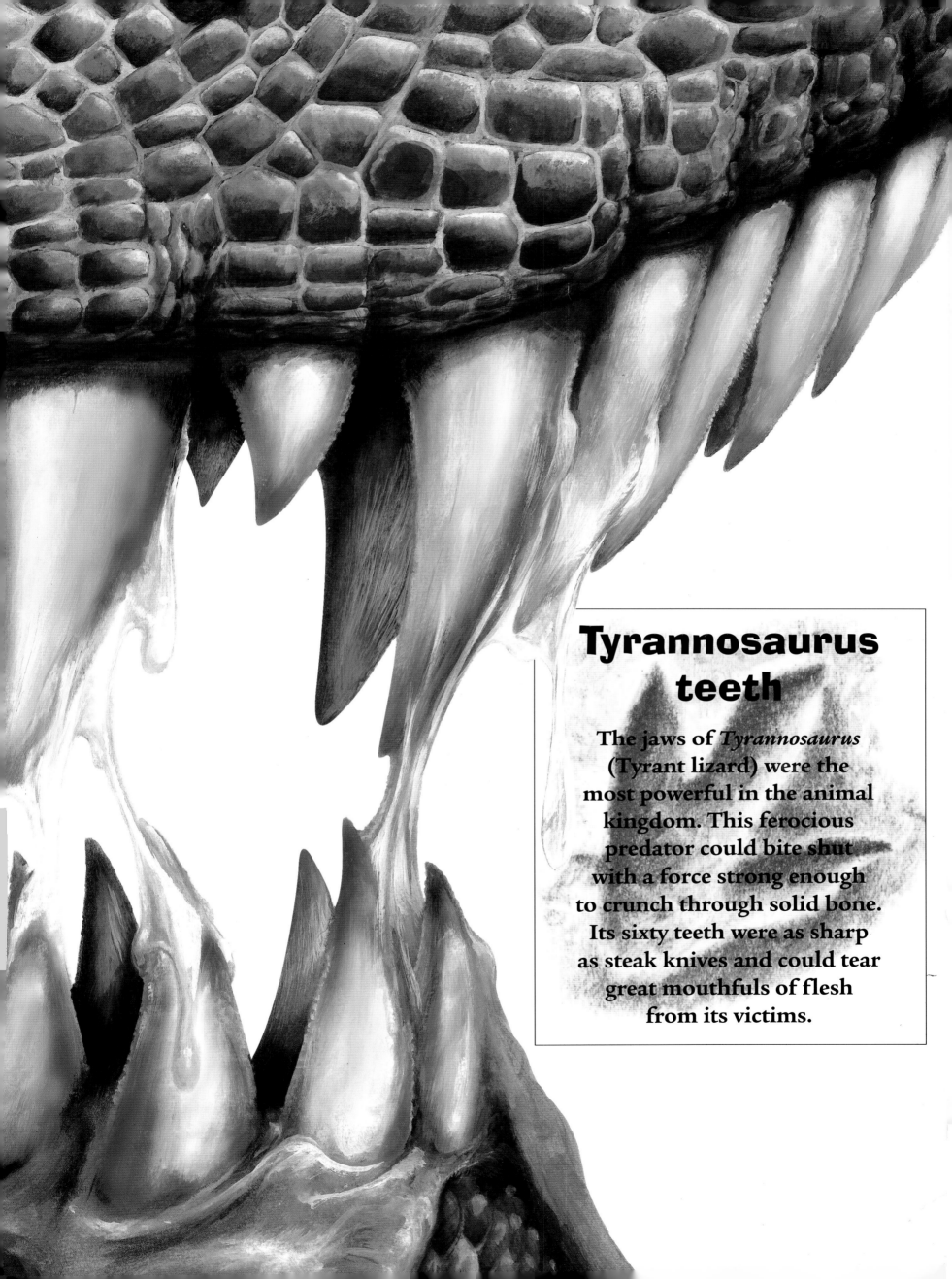

Tyrannosaurus teeth

The jaws of *Tyrannosaurus* (Tyrant lizard) were the most powerful in the animal kingdom. This ferocious predator could bite shut with a force strong enough to crunch through solid bone. Its sixty teeth were as sharp as steak knives and could tear great mouthfuls of flesh from its victims.

A slow death...

It wasn't just the sheer size and power of *Tyrannosaurus* that made it so deadly! *T-rex* teeth had a row of tiny serrations along the edges. Shreds of meat became trapped between these serrations, where it rotted. Once prey was bitten, even if it managed to escape, the wound would quickly have become infected. The victim would have died of blood poisoning – killed by the bacteria in the teeth that had bitten it.

LIFE-SIZE

Oviraptor

Scary chicken

Oviraptor may look like a chicken, but it was actually a fierce, Cretaceous meat eater that fed on small mammals, lizards and even young dinosaurs! Unlike most meat-eating dinosaurs, *Oviraptor* had two strange, tooth-like bumps in the roof of its mouth, which it may have used for cracking eggs (its name means "Egg thief").

Common fossils

Ammonites belonged to the family of mollusks that includes the squid. Ammonites became extinct at the same time as the mosasaurs and the dinosaurs.

Squid-like ammonites were typical prey for mosasaurs, such as Platecarpus. *Mosasaurs were large ocean-living lizards that appeared late in the dinosaur age.*

Dangerous seas

Going for a swim in the Cretaceous Period would have been pretty impossible! Lurking in the hidden depths of the seas were true ocean-dwelling carnivores. There were snake-necked plesiosaurs, sharp-toothed pliosaurs and fish-like ichthyosaurs. The top marine predators, however, were the enormous mosasaurs, such as *Tylosaurus* and the *Platecarpus.* These ever-hungry reptiles grew to 9 meters (30 feet) long and would have eaten fish as well as other, non-ocean living prey.

A *Pteranodon* is caught by the giant mosasaur, *Tylosaurus.*

Lasting giant

Turtles are real survivors. They were around when the dinosaurs' domination of the Earth began, and some two hundred million years later they are still with us – true "living fossils". At over 3.5 meters (12 feet) long, the huge Cretaceous turtle, *Archelon* was as big as a car and is the largest turtle found so far. Fossils of this marine giant are rare, which suggests that it wandered the oceans alone.

FIGHTING FIT

Just like animals today, the dinosaurs had to share one world, and many different species regularly came into contact with each other. Some dinosaurs got along with each other, others didn't! Fossils show us that some amazing fights occurred between animals – the plains of the Mesozoic era were quite a battlefield!

Pachycephalosaurus *was a bit of a bone-head! In spite of its large skull, its brain, (the small shape in the cross-section above) took up very little room. At its thickest the skull is an amazing 25 centimeters (8 ½ inches) thick.*

Wrestling giants

When animals of the same species fight each other, it is usually to defend their territory, or to decide which animal will rule the group and control the females. In the picture (above) a herd of *Dryosaurus* keep a watchful eye on two fighting *Diplodocus*. It is possible that long-necked sauropods such as dryosaurs "neck-wrestled", like today's giraffes.

Clash of the giants

The fossils of *Triceratops* (Three-horned face) show some unexpected details about this well-known dinosaur. Its skull was thicker over its brain and above the eyes, and its neck bones were extra strong to take the enormous impact when the animal charged. But which dinosaurs would have been on the receiving end of such an attack? Fights between *Triceratops* and *Tyrannosaurus* certainly took place, because *Triceratops* skulls have been found with the unmistakable teeth marks of *Tyrannosaurus* on them. Other *Triceratops* fossils show signs of wounds caused by the horns of another *Triceratops*. These would have been fierce battles!

Scarred fossil

Sometimes the signs of injuries on fossils tell us whether or not a wound would have killed an animal. The picture (below) shows that the left cheek bone of this fossilized *Triceratops* skull has been pierced through completely. Perhaps it was caused by the horns of another *Triceratops*. The way in which the bone continued to grow shows that the wound healed while the animal was still alive.

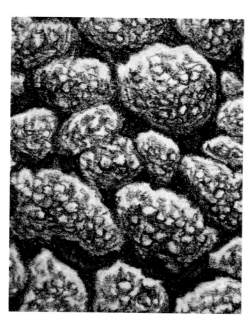

A strong back

This skeleton of *Triceratops* shows how the bones of the spine (vertebrae) are closer together above the animal's hips. This is also common in other large dinosaurs, and gave the skeletons of these heavy animals the extra strength they needed. A fully grown *Triceratops* would have weighed more than an elephant.

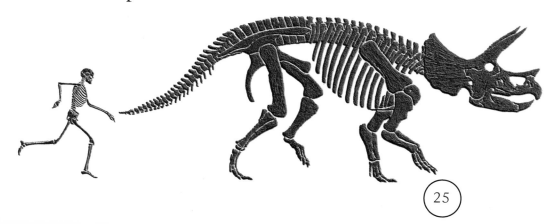

A fossil fragment of the tough skin of a Triceratops.

Head to head

One group of dinosaurs seems to have settled disputes head on. The pachycephalosaurs (thick-headed reptiles), which lived at the end of the Cretaceous Period, were plant eaters that had unusually strong, thick skulls. Their neck bones also seemed to have acted like shock absorbers. So just as rams today butt heads in clashes with rivals, it seems likely that these dinosaurs did the same. *Pachycephalosaurus* was the largest known type of pachycephalosaur. The smaller *Stegoceras* (Horn-roof) lacked nose spikes.

Pachycephalosaurus and Stegoceras

LIFE-SIZE

DINOSAUR CHAT

It's likely that some dinosaurs made sounds like a trombone or a bassoon. This happened when air from their lungs was blown out through hollow tubes in their crests. Dawn sounds in the Mesozoic era may have been a mix of hoots, honks and whistles. A true dinosaur chorus!

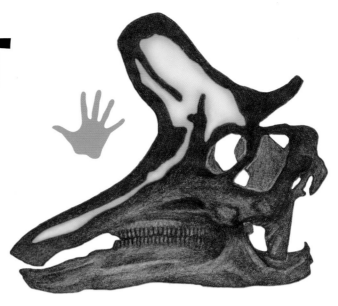

Air passages (shown in blue in the picture above) connected the crest of Lambeosaurus to the nostrils.

Hadrosaur orchestra!

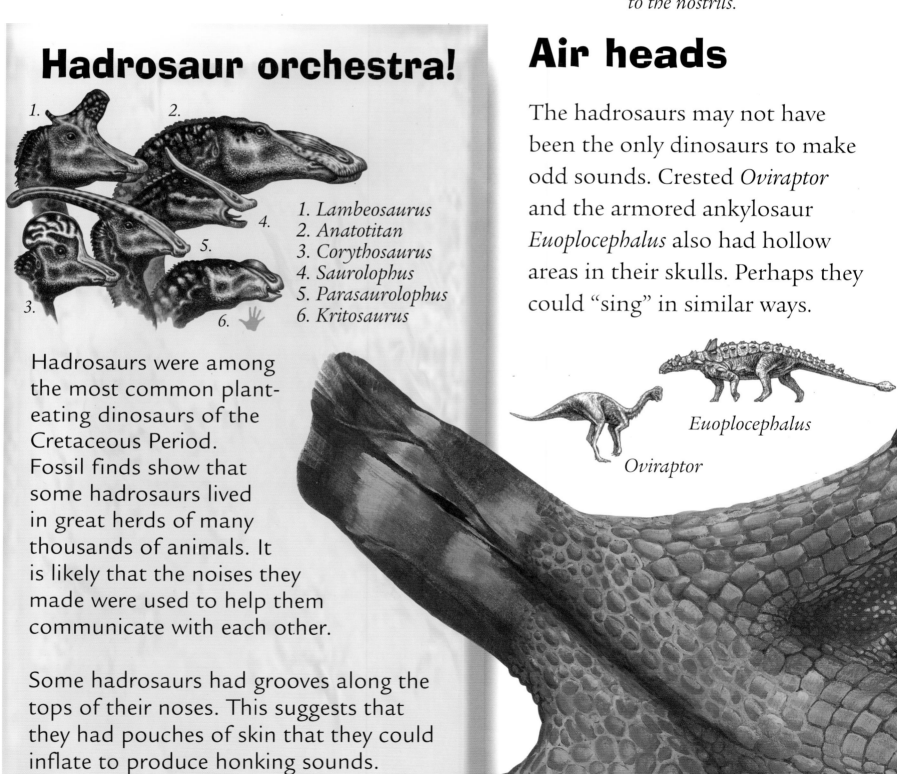

1. Lambeosaurus
2. Anatotitan
3. Corythosaurus
4. Saurolophus
5. Parasaurolophus
6. Kritosaurus

Hadrosaurs were among the most common plant-eating dinosaurs of the Cretaceous Period. Fossil finds show that some hadrosaurs lived in great herds of many thousands of animals. It is likely that the noises they made were used to help them communicate with each other.

Some hadrosaurs had grooves along the tops of their noses. This suggests that they had pouches of skin that they could inflate to produce honking sounds.

Air heads

The hadrosaurs may not have been the only dinosaurs to make odd sounds. Crested *Oviraptor* and the armored ankylosaur *Euoplocephalus* also had hollow areas in their skulls. Perhaps they could "sing" in similar ways.

Euoplocephalus

Oviraptor

CRESTS AND HORNS

Many meat-eating dinosaurs had horn-like crests or large ridges on their heads. These were probably used as signals, warning their rivals to stay away. If this failed they could always use their huge teeth and claws!

This rare fossil is half the skull of the crested carnivore Cryolophosaurus. *The grey areas show the parts which have been reconstructed.*

South Pole dinosaur

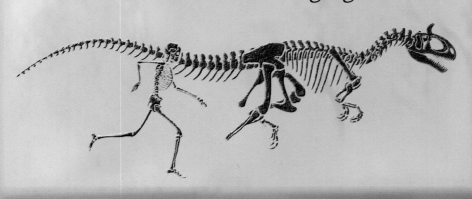

About one hundred and ninety million years ago, in the Early Jurassic Period, the Antarctic was closer to the equator than it is today so the climate was warmer. The landscape was a forest of ferns and pine trees. This was the hunting ground of *Cryolophosaurus* (Frozen-crested reptile). This predator had one of the most striking crests of any known carnivorous dinosaur. The crest spread out above its eyes like twin fan-shaped wings, and must have been a startling sight.

Horn defence

Plant-eating dinosaurs also had crests. The hadrosaurs were notorious for their different-shaped crested heads. Crest size and shape may have varied with the dinosaur's age. *Parasaurolophus* had a crest that was more than double the size of its skull. Many ceratopsians had horns on the nose and face. *Triceratops* had a nose horn that was similar to the horn of a rhinoceros. It also had a larger horn over each eye. In a clash with its deadly enemy *Tyrannosaurus*, it would have been hard for the predator to attack without getting hurt.

Hollow bones

An earlier relative of *Dilophosaurus* was the smaller *Coelophysis* from the Triassic Period. Its name means "Hollow form", and refers to its hollow bones; a feature that it shared both with *Dilophosaurus* and with all other meat-eating dinosaurs. However, although their bones were hollow, meat eaters were much stronger than plant eaters to help them survive their tougher, more violent lifestyle.

Color confusion

Fossils cannot tell us what color an animal was, so the colors used for dinosaur reconstructions are always imaginary. But if the crest of the hadrosaur *Lambeosaurus* (below) was used as a signal to other hadrosaurs, then it probably had some very striking and colorful markings.

Two or four?

Lambeosaurus, like other hadrosaurs, moved easily on two legs as well as on four. How it moved depended on how fast it wanted to go and how high it needed to reach.

LIFE-SIZE

Crested heads

The horns and crests on these meat-eating dinosaurs (dark brown) are actually bones on the skull. It's possible that these features on living dinosaurs were made of a hard covering (the same material as your fingernails), just as with today's horned mammals. Paleontologists call these various lumps and bumps on dinosaurs "rugosities", meaning "wrinkles".

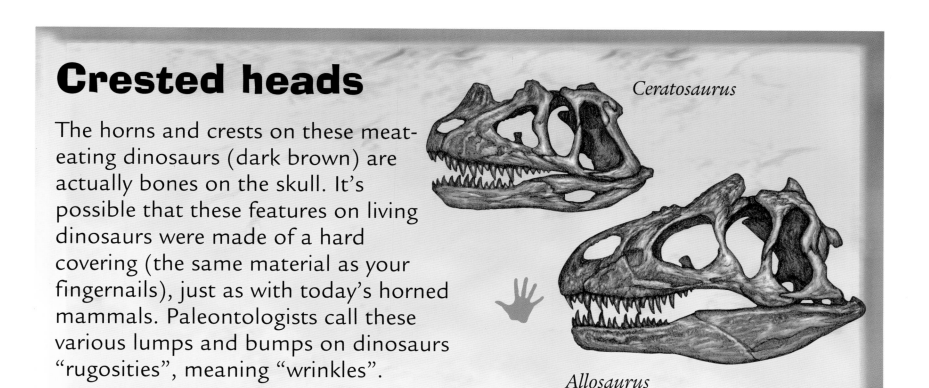

Ceratosaurus

Allosaurus

Horned hunters

Carnotaurus means "Flesh-eating bull" and takes its name from the two bull-like horns above its eyes. It had tiny forelimbs which were so small that the hands seemed to grow right from its body. *Majungatholus* (Majunga-dome) lived towards the end of the Cretaceous Period. It had a single short horn on top of its head, above the eyes, and a second raised ridge of bone behind the horn.

Fossils of Majungatholus *(below left) have been found in Madagascar, an island off the east coast of Africa. Fossils of* Carnotaurus *(below right) have been found in South America.*

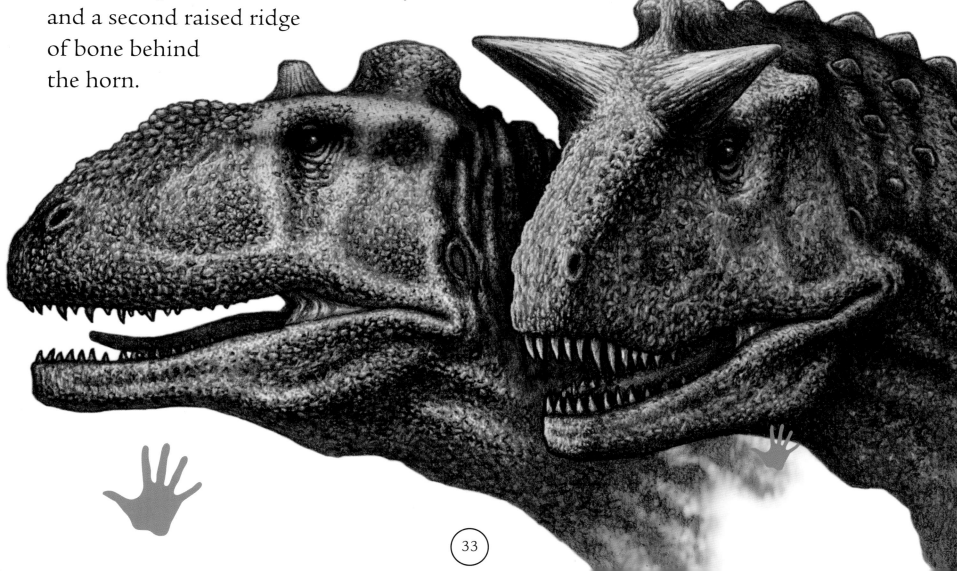

Jurassic terror

There are several odd features about *Dilophosaurus*, which has been called the "Terror of the Early Jurassic Period". It had extremely long teeth, but a very weak jaw. Its double crest is very striking, but it was not strong enough to use for fighting, so was probably used for display to attract a mate.

LIFE-SIZE

Dilophosaurus

SCENES FROM LOST WORLDS

As well as skeleton fossils, there are other kinds of fossils that give us vital information. These are called "trace fossils" and they include footprints, tracks and droppings. All these remains help us to build a picture of the world in which the dinosaurs lived.

Fossils of footprints reveal how heavy a dinosaur was and how quickly it moved.

Trace of the past

Trace fossils include gastroliths (stomach stones), teeth marks (which, when found on fossil bones, may indicate either feeding or fighting), nests, and even coprolites, a word used by paleontologists to describe fossilized dinosaur dung. Not only can coprolites offer clues to what dinosaurs ate, but sometimes they might even contain the burrows of Mesozoic dung beetles – a case of trace fossils inside other trace fossils!

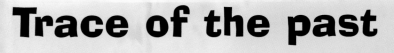

gastrolith

Tyrannosaurus toilet!

A recent find in Canada, shown life-size below, is a massive, 44 centimeter-long (17 in) fossil. It contained what appears to be the crunched-up neck shield of a young *Triceratops*. This king-sized coprolite (fossilized dinosaur dung) was almost certainly produced by a *Tyrannosaurus*.

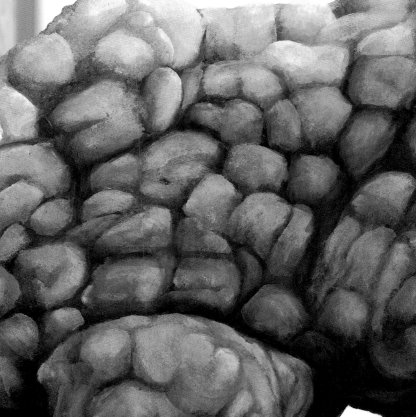

Travelling together

Fossilized bones can tell us a great deal about what a dinosaur looked like, but dinosaur footprints can tell us lots of other things. Was the dinosaur travelling alone or with a group? Was it walking on two legs or on four? Was it ambling along slowly or running quickly, or maybe even being hunted? These and other questions can be answered by studying trackways – sets of fossil footprints which together form a trail.

Sauropod and human footprints. We know these Jurassic sauropods travelled in groups by studying their trackways.

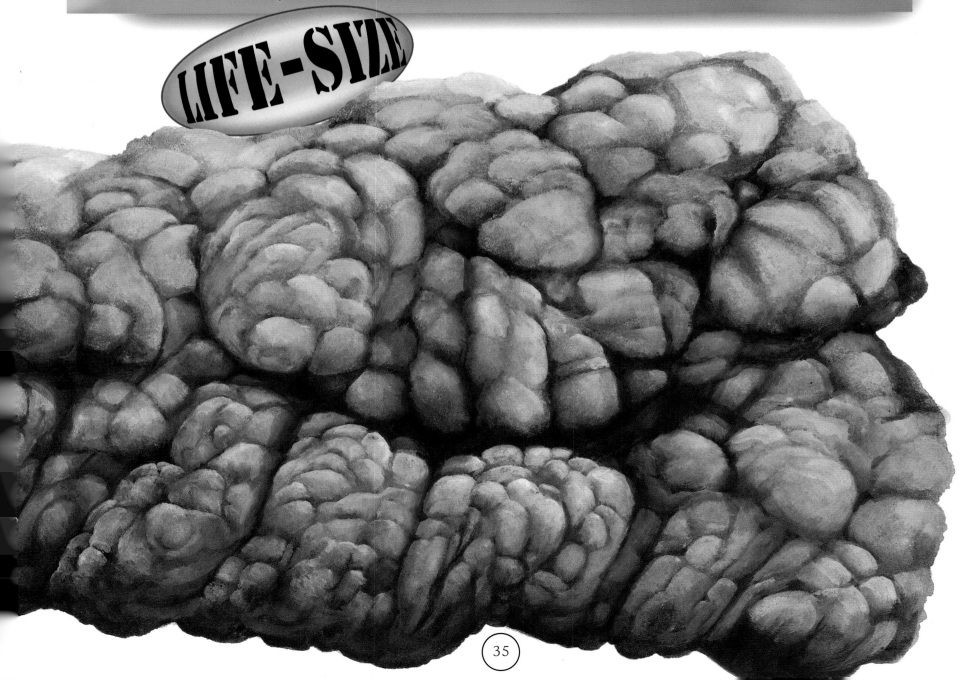

LIFE-SIZE

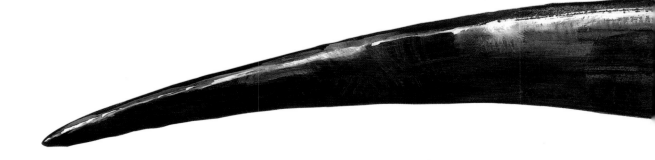

The claws of
Therizinosaurus

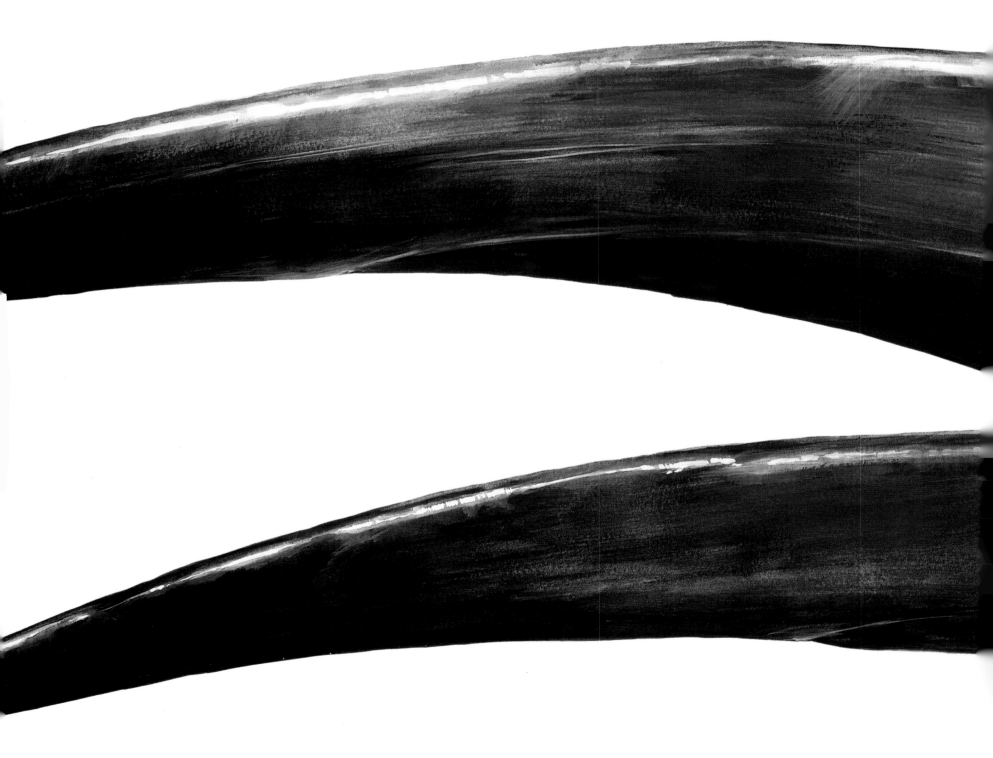

Dinosaur oddball

Just about everything to do with the Cretaceous dinosaur *Therizinosaurus* (Scythe lizard) is rather strange. In fact, it looks as if it's made up of body parts from lots of different dinosaurs. *Therizinosaurus* had a long neck and a plump body with feathers, and huge claws that grew up to 1 meter (3 feet) in length. But this dinosaur was not a fierce predator. Instead it lived on leaves and shoots and used its scary claws to pull juicy vegetation down to eat.

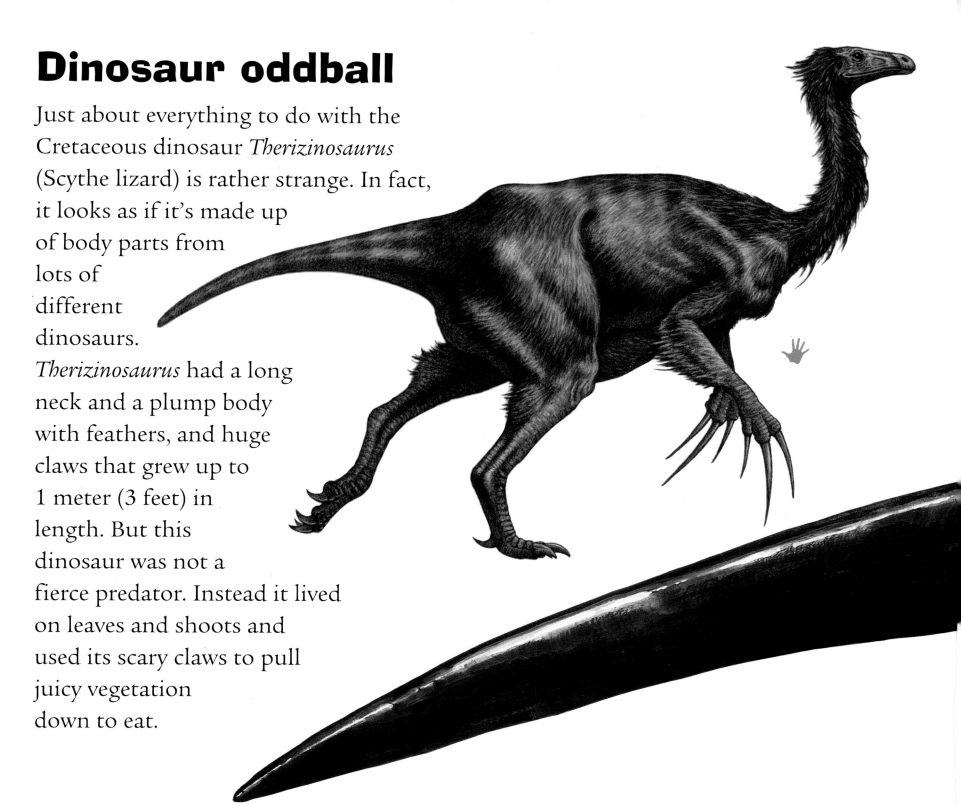

Ancient food

This enormous trace fossil of a termite mound may have been one possible source of food for therizinosaurs. Perhaps, like anteaters of today, they used their long, thin claws to break open such mounds and eat the termites that lived inside.

FIGHT FOR SURVIVAL!

Carnivorous (meat-eating) dinosaurs were fast, powerful killers. They hunted herbivores (plant eaters) and other dinosaurs that were often bigger than themselves. This meant that the hunters needed successful ways of killing their prey and the hunted needed effective methods of defense. As the dinosaurs evolved, so they developed more deadly claws, longer and sharper spikes, and thicker and harder skin, which they used in a variety of dramatic ways as they all fought to survive.

Fighting back

Euoplocephalus was covered in hard plates, bony studs and spikes. It even had an extra disk of bone covering its eyelids which made it a powerful opponent in any fight. In this picture *Euoplocephalus* is using its tail in a battle against a *Tyrannosaurus*. It probably turned its back on its attacker and swung its heavy tail from side-to-side before whiplashing it with a mighty blow.

Tough tails

Some plant-eating dinosaurs used their own tails as defensive weapons. *Euoplocephalus* (True-plated head), which lived during the Late Cretaceous Period, had a long tail with a large "club" at the end filled with spongy tissue that made it both strong and springy. The *Stegosaurus* (Roof lizard), which lived during the Late Jurassic Period, had rows of thick plates along its back and four long, sharp spikes at the end of its tail.

Skeletons of Euoplocephalus (top) *and* Stegosaurus (bottom).

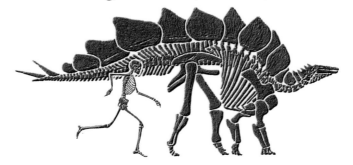

Cretaceous killers

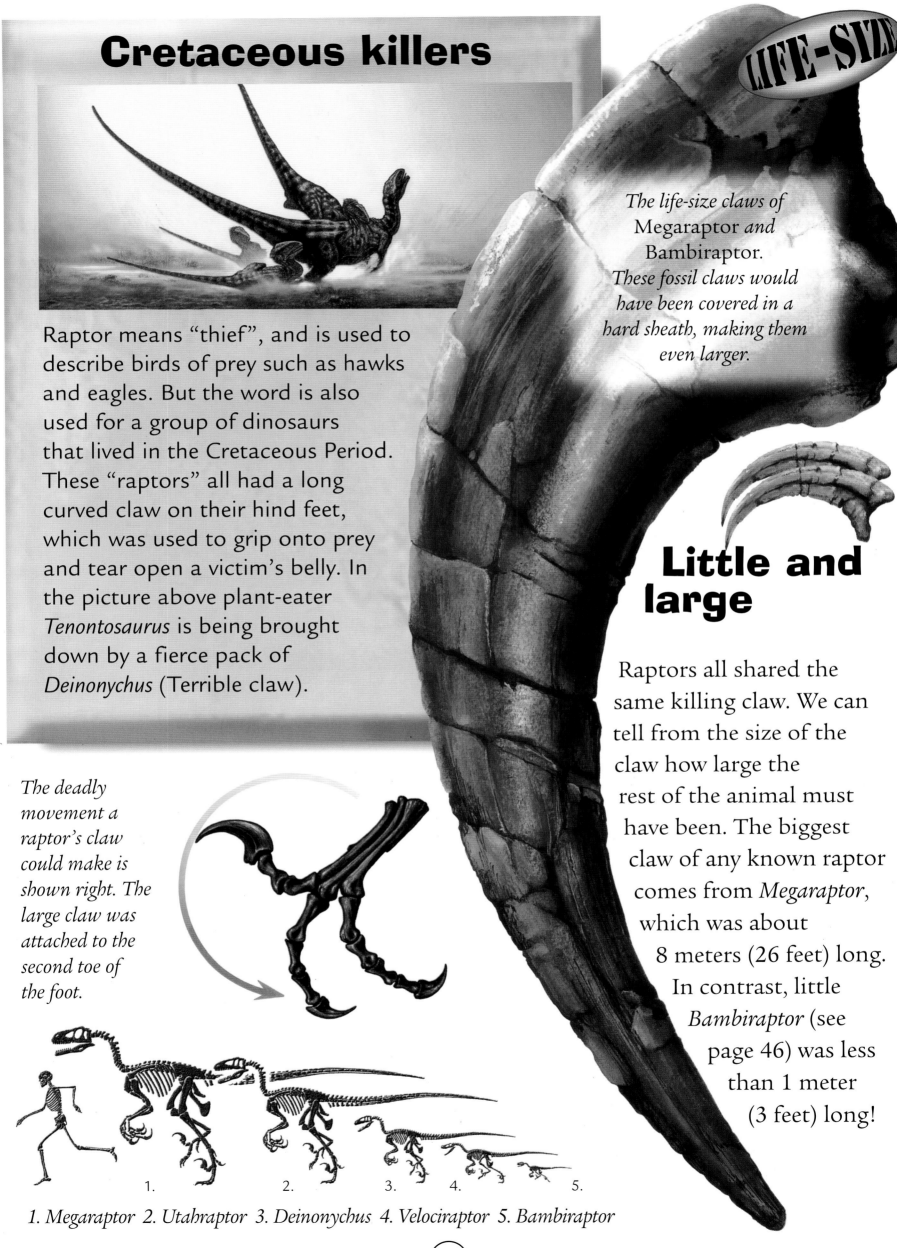

Raptor means "thief", and is used to describe birds of prey such as hawks and eagles. But the word is also used for a group of dinosaurs that lived in the Cretaceous Period. These "raptors" all had a long curved claw on their hind feet, which was used to grip onto prey and tear open a victim's belly. In the picture above plant-eater *Tenontosaurus* is being brought down by a fierce pack of *Deinonychus* (Terrible claw).

The life-size claws of Megaraptor *and* Bambiraptor. *These fossil claws would have been covered in a hard sheath, making them even larger.*

Little and large

Raptors all shared the same killing claw. We can tell from the size of the claw how large the rest of the animal must have been. The biggest claw of any known raptor comes from *Megaraptor*, which was about 8 meters (26 feet) long. In contrast, little *Bambiraptor* (see page 46) was less than 1 meter (3 feet) long!

The deadly movement a raptor's claw could make is shown right. The large claw was attached to the second toe of the foot.

1.   2.   3.   4.   5.

1. Megaraptor 2. Utahraptor 3. Deinonychus 4. Velociraptor 5. Bambiraptor

Sharp claws

Therizinosaurus means "Scythe lizard", because its huge claws look like the blades of a scythe, a tool that was once used for mowing fields. The fossil of *Therizinosaurus* was found where there were once many rivers, so perhaps it waded into the water to catch fish.

LAST TO BE BORN

Fossil evidence shows that dinosaurs hatched from eggs, like today's birds. So even the fiercest of dinosaurs cared for and raised their young. Dinosaur eggs were very small compared to their enormous bodies. Huge eggs would have had thick shells that the baby dinosaurs would have found impossible to break open. The two dinosaurs pictured here, *Edmontosaurus* (Edmonton lizard) and *Tyrannosaurus*, were among the last of the dinosaurs as they lived right at the end of the Cretaceous Period.

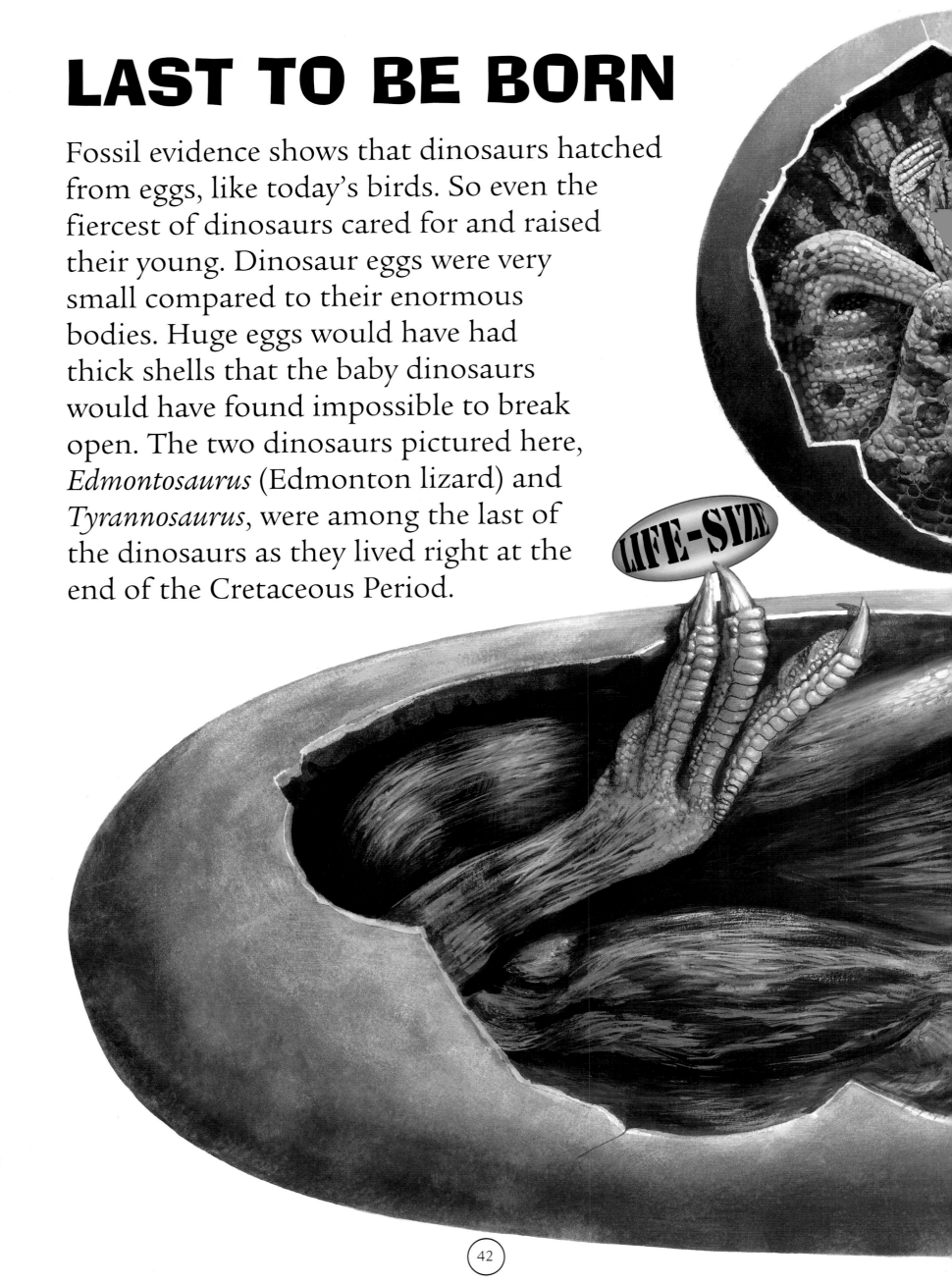

LIFE-SIZE

The hunter and the hunted

Like all eggshells, dinosaur eggs had tiny holes, called pores, which let air in and out. These allowed the baby to breathe while it developed inside the egg. The first and biggest fossilized dinosaur eggs found belonged to *Hypselosaurus*. These eggs are 30 centimeters (1 foot) long, 25 centimeters(10 inches) wide and may have weighed about 7 kilograms (15 pounds). The two dinosaurs seen here life-size have yet to be born. The baby in the round egg is the plant-eating hadrosaur *Edmontosaurus*. Below it in the long egg is a *Tyrannosaurus* baby.

Unborn Edmontosaurus *(left) and* Tyrannosaurus *(below).*

Dino nest

The dinosaur eggs in this nest have been fossilized exactly as they were laid, in an outward-spiralling cluster. The fossils of lizards have sometimes been found near such nests – perhaps the lizards were attempting to steal the eggs to eat.

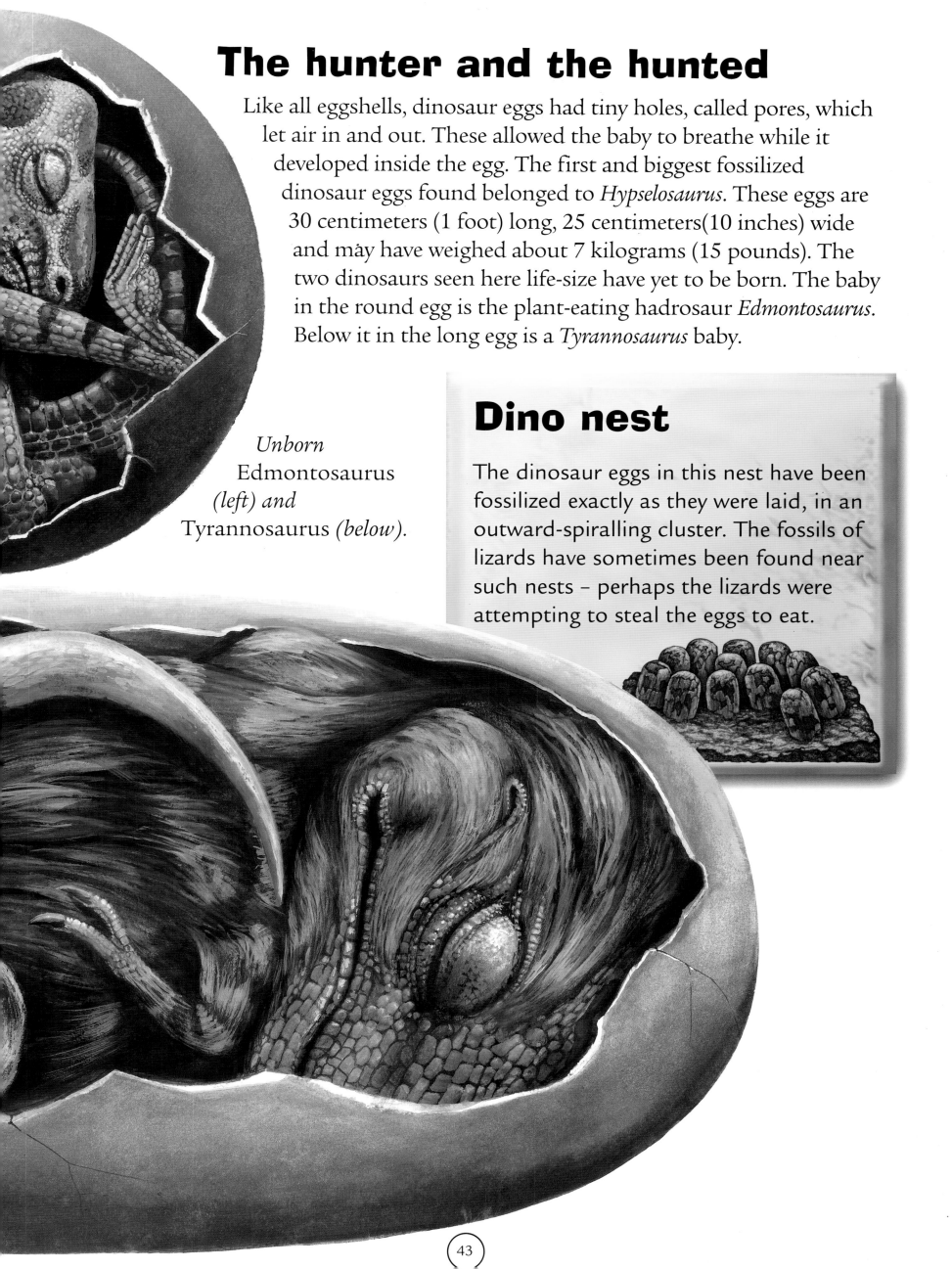

VANISHING ACT

Dinosaurs survived for an astonishing one hundred and sixty million years. Throughout this time they constantly evolved to cope with changes in the world around them. So why did they become extinct? Was there a sudden change in their environment, or were there other factors involved?

The crystals in this sample are pointing in different directions. Only a tremendous explosion could have caused this to happen. This piece of evidence of an Earth-shaking impact occurred at the same time that dinosaurs became extinct.

Extinction theories

At the end of the Mesozoic era almost three quarters of life on Earth died. Most scientists now agree that two things may have caused the mass extinction. First the climate had been gradually cooling down. Second, around sixty-five million years ago something catastrophic happened – such as a huge comet striking the Earth.

End of an era

The end of the dinosaurs may have been very dramatic. There are many clues around the world that point to a catastrophic event happening some sixty-five million years ago. This is the time when all dinosaur fossils disappeared from the rocks. The most popular theory is that a huge meteorite or comet struck the Earth causing a chain of destructive events, including massive sea waves, great fires and extreme climate change. It may have created a gigantic cloud of dust that would have stopped sunlight reaching the Earth, causing animals and plants to die and become extinct. The picture above shows what a large sea wave might have looked like.

The fossil skull of the "duck-billed" hadrosaur Edmontosaurus – one of the last dinosaurs to have lived.

This tiny mammal Purgatorius, seen here life-size, lived in the Late Cretaceous Period. It survived the mass extinction at the end of the Mesozoic era. It is one of the first ancestors of human beings.

A new beginning

Reptiles such as crocodiles, lizards, snakes and turtles, which lived alongside the dinosaurs, remain with us today. The deaths of the dinosaurs, marine reptiles and winged pterosaurs created new opportunities for other animal survivors. From the beginning of the new era, the Cenozoic era, tiny mammals also flourished. These mammals evolved into many new forms and eventually dominated the Earth. Some returned to the sea to evolve into the whales and dolphins of today. Yet it would be another sixty million years before the first humans appeared. Although humans have been the dominant life form on Earth for some four million years, this is nothing compared to the hundred and sixty million years that the dinosaurs had managed!

Almost a near miss...

It is thought that the giant crater off the coast of Mexico is the spot where a meteorite or comet landed. This may have started the chain of events that lead to the dinosaurs' extinction. The picture opposite shows that the crater may have been formed by the comet gouging out a deep trench as it landed, instead of slamming down directly. This suggests that the comet striking the Earth was almost a "near miss" event. Just how different would things be today had the object missed the Earth? Would dinosaurs rule the world, while tiny mammals scuttled by, still waiting for their chance at world domination?

The crater under the sea. The trench is shown in blue.

Is it a bird...?

Microraptor (Little thief) is the smallest known dinosaur. *Microraptor* is important because, as with the fossil of its feathered relative *Sinornithosaurus* (see box below), its fossil also shows evidence of a feather-like covering. Both dinosaurs were dromaeosaurs, a group of dinosaurs that also includes the raptors *Velociraptor* and *Bambiraptor*. The dromaeosaurs were the most bird-like of all dinosaurs. It is now believed that *Microraptor* had much larger wings than that shown below.

LIFE-SIZE

Microraptor

Feathered dino

This fossil dinosaur is one of the most unique ever found. It shows a Chinese bird reptile, and is so well-preserved that a feather-like covering can be seen on the fossil.

Bird-like killer

Bambiraptor (Baby raider) was a pint-sized dinosaur that looked very similar to a bird. Like all raptors, its scythe-like claws made it a dangerous predator. It would probably have preyed upon lizards, frogs and other small creatures that lived in the Late Cretaceous Period, some seventy-two million years ago.

The last dinosaurs

It's not easy to tell whether rocks in one place on Earth are a little bit younger or older than rocks in other places. So, we are not sure if some dinosaurs outlived others thousands of miles away. Certainly, the last dinosaur groups included *Tyrannosaurus* and *Triceratops*. Bone-headed *Stygimoloch* from the pachycephalosaur family, found in Montana, may have been one of the last dinosaurs to survive. But only a few pieces of broken skull have been found. All large marine reptiles – the mosasaurs and plesiosaurs, as well as flying reptiles, such as the pterosaurs – disappeared with the dinosaurs.

A feather may provide living contact with the long-vanished world of the dinosaurs.

First bird

Archaeopteryx (Ancient wing) has often been called the first bird, but it also had features from its dinosaur ancestors, such as its carnivore teeth and a long bony tail. Birds have a large breastbone to hold the strong chest muscles, which they use to beat their wings. Although the breastbone of *Archaeopteryx* was not as big as later birds, it was larger than that of a non-flying animal.

Birds – modern-day dinosaurs?

Birds evolved from small, meat-eating dinosaurs. It seems that feathers developed first for keeping the dinosaur's body warm. Long wing feathers may have evolved to help the little dinosaur to catch flying prey like insects. The power of flight would have come later.

INDEX

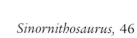

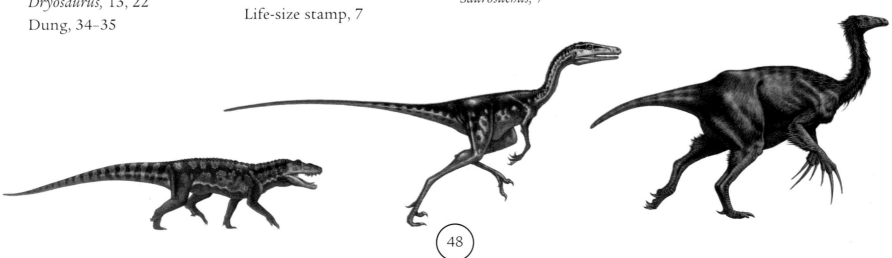